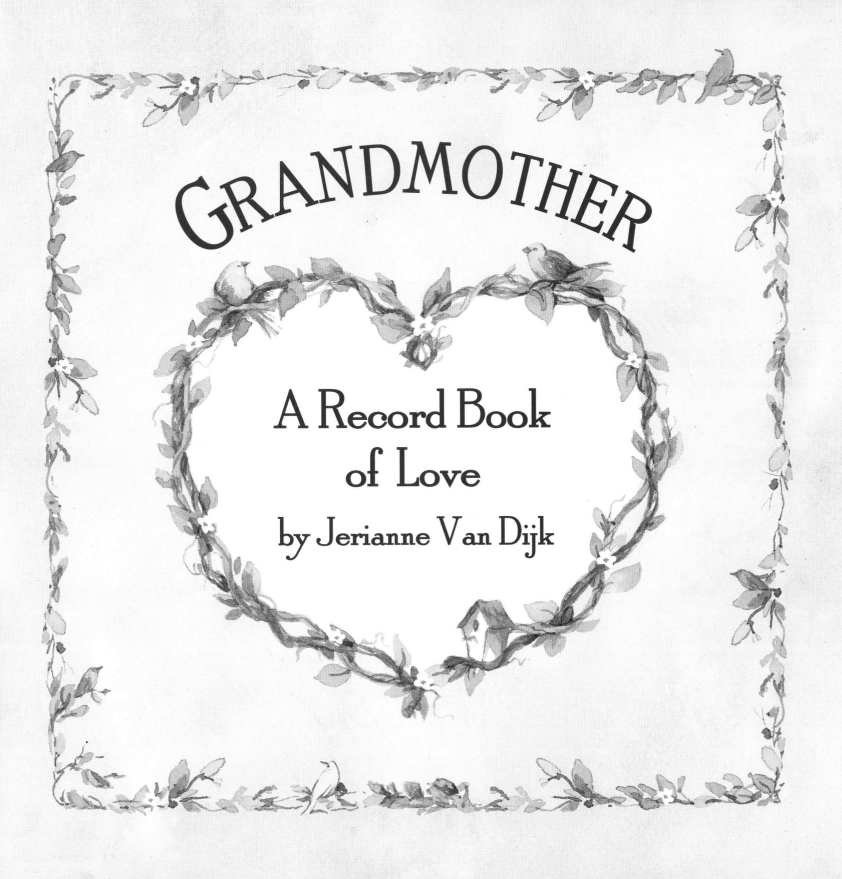

GRANDMOTHER

A Record Book of Love

by Jerianne Van Dijk

©1999 Havoc Publishing
ISBN 1-57977-133-5

Published by Havoc Publishing • San Diego, California
Design ©1998 Jerianne Van Dijk

Please write to us for more information on
Havoc Publishing products.

Havoc Publishing
6330 Nancy Ridge Drive, Suite 104
San Diego, CA 92121

Grandmother

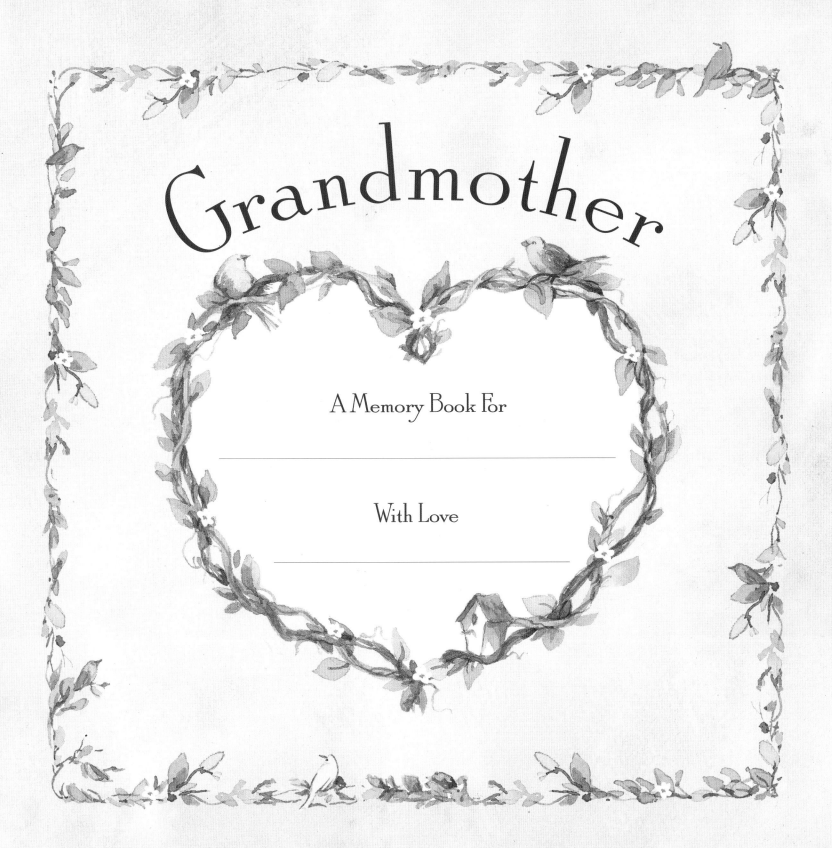

A Memory Book For

_____

With Love

_____

Contents

All About Me

My Family Tree

Family History

Photographs

Memorable Stories

The Early Days

History in the Making

School Days

Best Friends

As a Young Woman

Photographs

Proud Moments

My Philosophy

Photographs

Contents

The Best of Times

Grandfather

Getting Married

From My Kitchen

Photographs

Starting a Family

Thoughts & Wishes

Grandchildren

Watching the Grandkids Grow

Family Holidays

Events & Traditions

Travels

The Future

My maiden name is

I was named after

My birth date is

My birth place was

All About Me

My Family Tree

Great - Grandmother

_____

Great - Grandfather

_____

Great - Grandfather

_____

Great - Grandmother

_____

Grandfather

_____

Grandmother

_____

Mother

_____

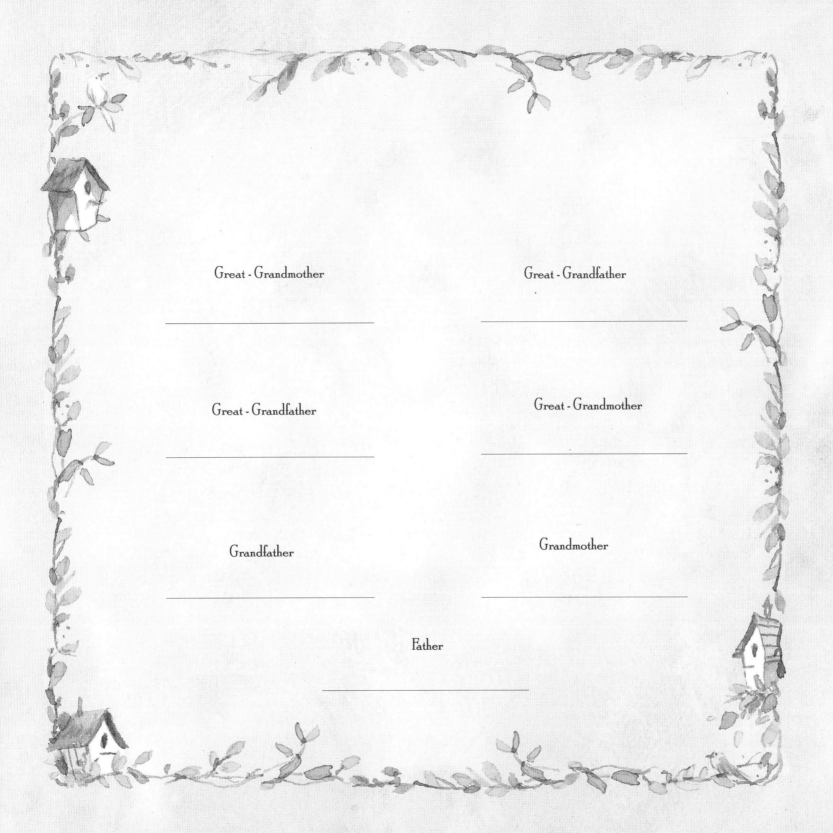

Great - Grandmother

_____

Great - Grandfather

_____

Great - Grandfather

_____

Great - Grandmother

_____

Grandfather

_____

Grandmother

_____

Father

_____

Family History

Family Photograph

Photograph

Photograph

Memorable Stories

Favorite Hobbies

_____

_____

_____

_____

_____

Favorite Playmates

_____

_____

_____

_____

_____

The Early Days

My earliest memories

_____

_____

_____

_____

My fondest memories

_____

_____

_____

_____

As a child I liked to

_____

_____

_____

History in the Making

Most memorable President

_____

_____

Famous scandals

_____

_____

Important issues at the time

_____

_____

Local issues

_____

National issues

_____

_____

Around the world

_____

_____

Famous movie stars _____

_____

_____

Famous musicians/singers _____

_____

Favorite radio shows _____

_____

Music we danced to _____

_____

_____

_____

Photograph

Photograph

My favorite story about growing up

School Days

Where I went to school _____

_____

_____

Extracurricular activities I participated in _____

_____

_____

What I excelled at _____

_____

My favorite thing about school was _____

_____

My favorite subjects _____

_____

_____

My least favorite subjects _____

_____

_____

My favorite teacher(s) _____

_____

_____

My least favorite teacher(s) _____

_____

_____

Best Friends

Name _____

How we met _____

_____

How long we've know each other _____

_____

Best Friends

Name
_____

How we met
_____

_____

How long we've know each other
_____

_____

My Favorite Poem

As a Young Woman

I would dream of _____

_____

_____

_____

_____

_____

_____

_____

_____

Photograph

Photograph

Proud Moments

I was proud of _____

_____

_____

_____

_____

_____

_____

Photograph

My Philosophy

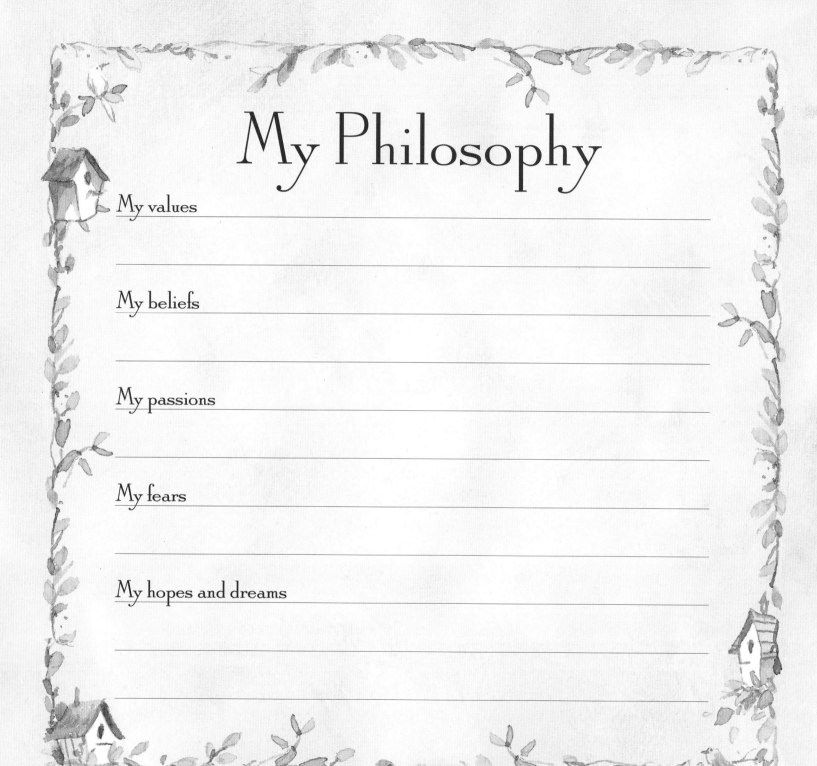

My values

_____

_____

My beliefs

_____

_____

My passions

_____

_____

My fears

_____

_____

My hopes and dreams

_____

_____

_____

Words of wisdom

Photograph

Photograph

Photograph

I remember when

The Best of Times

Birthdays

_____

_____

Celebrations

_____

_____

Get-togethers

_____

_____

Family vacations

_____

_____

_____

_____

Grandfather

Grandpa's family members _____

_____

Where they are from _____

_____

_____

How we met _____   Our first date _____

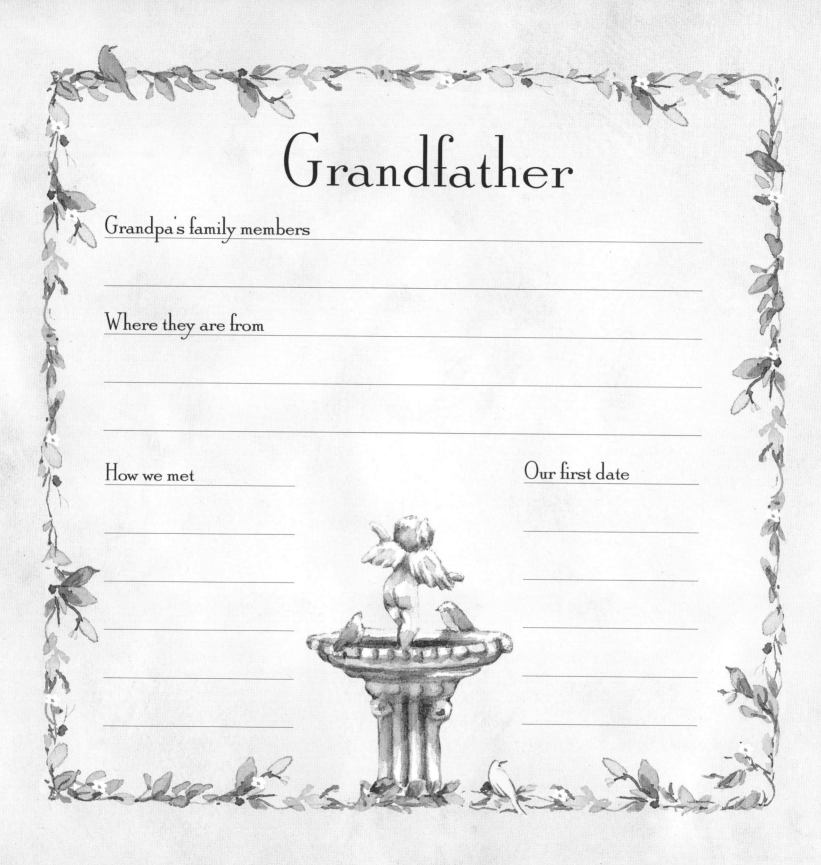

Photograph

Photograph

Getting Married

Our Wedding Day

_____

_____

Ceremony location

_____

_____

Reception location

_____

_____

Special people who attended

_____

_____

Where we honeymooned

_____

_____

Wedding Day

Photograph

Photograph

_____
Date

Our first house

Changes and fix-ups

Price

Our neighborhood

Our friends

Photograph of our first home

From My Kitchen

My favorite foods

_____

_____

_____

_____

_____

_____

How I learned to cook

_____

_____

_____

_____

Favorite Recipe

(Baking)

_____

_____

_____

_____

_____

_____

_____

Favorite Recipe

(Baking)

_____

_____

_____

_____

_____

_____

_____

Favorite Recipe

(Cooking)

_____

_____

_____

_____

_____

_____

_____

Favorite Recipe

(Cooking)

_____

_____

_____

_____

_____

_____

_____

Favorite Recipe

(Holiday)

_____

_____

_____

_____

_____

_____

_____

_____

Favorite Recipe

(Holiday)

_____

_____

_____

_____

_____

_____

_____

_____

Photograph

Photograph

Children's Names

Starting a Family

When we decided to start a family
_____

_____

Who we told first
_____

_____

Pregnancy memories
_____

_____

_____

When the children were born
_____

_____

_____

Thoughts & Wishes

Thoughts and wishes for our growing children
_____

_____

_____

_____

_____

_____

_____

_____

_____

Family
Photograph

Grandchildren

Signatures of grandchildren

Watching the Grandkids Grow

Favorite things to do at grandma's house _____

_____

_____

_____

_____

Distinct personalities _____

_____

_____

_____

_____

Family Holidays

Favorite holidays
_____
_____
_____
_____
_____
_____
_____
_____
_____
_____
_____

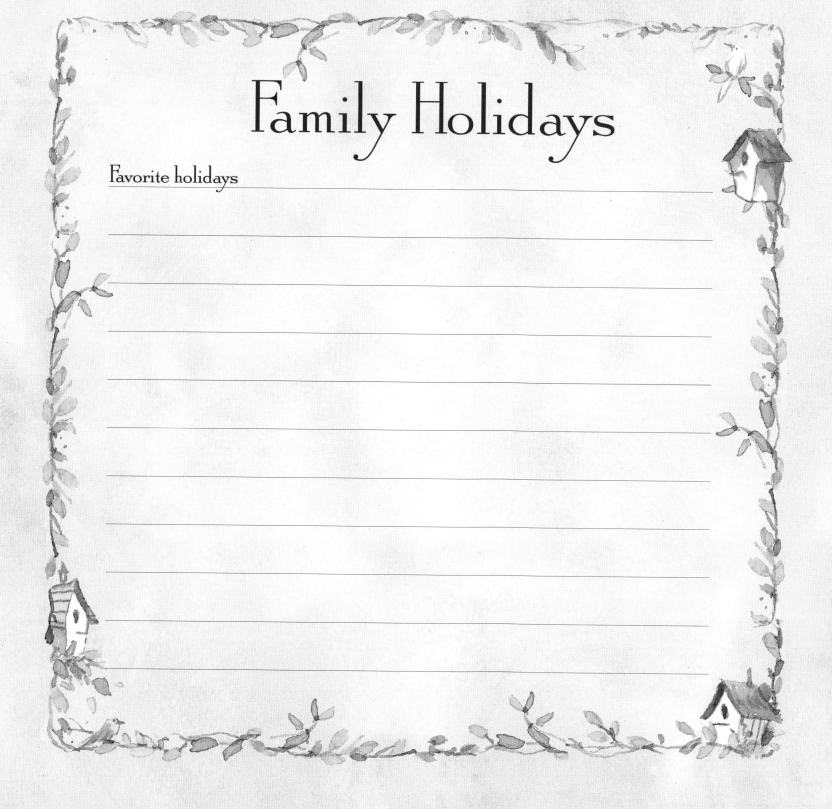

Events & Traditions

Special events in our family

_____

_____

_____

_____

_____

_____

_____

_____

_____

Special traditions we love to share

_____

_____

_____

_____

_____

_____

_____

_____

_____

Photograph

Photograph

Travels

Different places I've been _____

_____

_____

_____

The most exotic place I've been _____

_____

_____

Favorite cities _____

_____

_____

_____

Favorite landmarks _____

_____

_____

The Future

Available Record Books from Havoc

Baby
Coach
College Life
Couples
Dad
Family
Forever Friends
Girlfriends
Golf
Grandmother
Grandparents

Mom
Mothers &
Daughters
My Pregnancy
Our Honeymoon
Retirement
School Days
Single Life
Sisters
Teacher
Traveling
Adventures
Tying the Knot

Please write to us with your ideas for
additional Havoc Publishing products

Havoc Publishing
6330 Nancy Ridge Drive, Suite 104
San Diego, CA 92121